Christine Marendon (1964–) grew up bilingual (German and Italian), studied Italian in Erlangen and Siena, and graduated in 1999 with a thesis on Italian women writers in the nineteenth century. After working as a translator and publicist for some years in her native Bavaria, she now lives in Hamburg where she works with children with special needs.

Ken Cockburn (1960–) is a poet and translator based in Edinburgh, where he worked for many years at the Scottish Poetry Library. He was the first writer-in-residence at the John Murray Archive, National Library of Scotland, and was awarded the Arts Foundation Fellowship for Literary Translation 2008. A selection of his translations of contemporary German poems appeared as *Feathers and Lime*, while *Snapdragon* collects his versions of Arne Rautenberg's poems. His own collections include *Souvenirs and Homelands*, *On the flyleaf*, *The Road North* (with Alec Finlay) and *Floating the Woods*.

T0159809

Heroines from Abroad

poems

. . . .

CHRISTINE
MARENDON

translated by
KEN COCKBURN

. . . .

CARCANET

First published in Great Britain in 2018
by
Carcanet Press Limited
Alliance House, 30 Cross Street
Manchester M2 7AQ

Original poems in German © Christine Marendon, 2018.
Selection and translations © Ken Cockburn, 2018.

Book design: Luke Allan. Printed by SRP Ltd.
. A CIP catalogue record for this book is available from
the British Library, ISBN 9781784106300.

The publisher acknowledges financial assistance
from Arts Council England.

MIX
Paper from
responsible sources
FSC
www.fsc.org   FSC® C014540

Supported using public funding by
ARTS COUNCIL
ENGLAND

CONTENTS

Heroines from Abroad

NACH REGENGÜSSEN

Im milden, meerfeuchten Klima entstehen freundliche
Beziehungen zwischen dem Himmel, der mit jedem
Windstoß gelbe Wolken entführt, und den Mitteln
von Erde, Wasser, Luft und Licht. So wissen wir
was ein Baum wirklich ist, was seine Gestalt
bestimmt, warum er ein hohes Alter erreicht.
Seine immergrüne Beständigkeit folgt einer
festgelegten Anordnung des Weltbaubüros, aber
er neigt sich nach unten. Ob sich nun Menschen
gegenüberstehen, oder Gesetze: die Bänder
vollführen Drehungen durch alle Stockwerke
hindurch. Ein bei uns offenbar aussterbender
Rhythmus wirkt sich aus im Gefüge. Ebenso
wie die Kugel des Apfels in der Krone ihres
Trägers ruht: die Erde braucht sie doch.
Es gibt also wieder eine Drehung, sie dient ihr
als Segel. Und liegt nicht die Seele der Welt
in der Aufeinanderfolge von Blatt und Lücke?

AFTER RAINFALL

In mild, sea-humid climates friendly
relations arise between sky, which at each
breath of wind elopes with yellow clouds, and
the resources of earth, water, air and light. So
we know what a tree really is, what determines
its form, why it attains a great age.
Its evergreen constancy follows stipulations
set by the Global Office for Building, but
it tends to bow down. Now whether humans
stand on the other side, or laws: the conveyor belts
complete their revolutions through each and every
storey. A rhythm which in us is clearly
dying out results in structure. Similarly
the apple pip rests in the crown of its
bearer: after all it needs the earth.
So there is another revolution, which serves as
its sail. And doesn't the soul of the world
reside in the sequence of leaf and gap?

ANEMOS

*Von allen Sinnen erzeugt das Phänomen der
Atmung den Ausbruch der menschlichen Stimme.
Nimm Stoff aus einer Handvoll Erde: Anemos
bedeutet Wind und Seele zugleich. Es ist seltsam
wie den Beziehungen des Menschen die Wandlung
der Körper zugrunde liegt. Dankbarkeit ist etwas
Natürliches. Dann kommen Säure und Kristalle,
Dornen und Schuppen. Als wüsste man, dass
so nahe der Durchsichtigkeit des Weltraums auch
Farbe als etwas Überwundenes zurückbleiben
muss. Im Verhältnis zu unserer Größe sind wir
dann am stärksten, wenn wir im Material
denken. Frei im Licht stehen können
und ausatmen, ist die erste und letzte
aller philosophischen Handlungen.*

ANEMOS

The phenomenon of breath produces from all the
senses the eruption of the human voice.
Take matter from a handful of earth: *anemos*
signifies both wind and soul. It's strange
how human relationships are rooted in physical
transformations. Gratitude is something
natural. Then come acids and crystals,
thorns and scales. As though one knew that
so close to the transparency of space even
colour is left behind as something
superceded. Relative to our size then we
are at our strongest when we think in terms of
material. To have the freedom to stand in light
and breathe out, is the first and last
of all philosophical movements.

NACHTKERZE

Es lebt in jedem Menschen
die jähe Tiefe. Dunkler als die Lichtnelke
die am Tag nach innen gedreht ist
vermag sie weite Flächen
mit Gold zu überziehen.
So sind wir, Tier und Mensch
auch Pflanzen, Abdrücke
der Steinkohlezeit. Wir sind
Ableger, gehören also zu jener Art
die mit Blütenstaub und Honig zahlt
und die neue Zeit noch erwartet.
Die Blumen, in deren Sprache
das Wort „Garten" fehlt
beugen sich nach vorn
in die neubeflogene Narbe.
Alles ist verbunden
mit dem Nichtgehören.

EVENING PRIMROSE

In each person there exists a sheer
drop. Darker than campion
which during the day turns inwards
it likes to spread gold
over broad expanses.
So we, animals and humans,
are also vegetation, layers
of the coal age. We are
offshoots, belonging to the species
which pays with pollen and honey
and still awaits the new age.
The flowers, whose language
lacks a word for 'garden',
bend forward into
the newly flighted scar.
Everything is connected
to not belonging.

VORKOMMEN

*Es vergehen viele Jahre, bis eine Stadt ihr Inneres
nach außen kehrt. Schon sehr früh siedeln dort
die wilden Arten, in ihren alten Tagen greifen Erde
Sonne und Wind in das Geschehen ein. Stein genügt
längst nicht mehr, um Mensch zu werden. Es war wohl
zierlichen Vogelspuren folgend, dass eine neue Art
des Sehens unseren einzigen Garten wie eine Blume
riechen machte. Knospen, die wir Augen nennen,
pflegen ihren Weg allein zu finden, alles andere
ergibt sich von selbst. Auf unserer Zunge, ganz still,
geschieht irrtümlich ein Blühen: Dieser neuen
seelischen Lust folgen salzhaltige Bilder, für einen
Augenblick werden wir Menschen. Weit im Kreis
herumzulaufen, davon verstehen wir viel. Kultur
ist nichts anderes als menschliche Hemmungslosigkeit.
Lust ist ebensosehr Zartheit wie Raumtrunkenheit.
Was muss der Mensch alles tun in der Welt. Wer nicht
daran glaubt, mag sich die Antwort selbst geben.*

OCURRENCE

Many years pass before a town turns itself
inside out. Early on the wild varieties
settle there, late in the day earth sun and wind
intervene in what happens. It's been a while since
stone sufficed to become human. It was really
by following the tracery of bird-tracks that
a new way of seeing made our only garden smell
like a flower. Buds, which we call eyes,
are used to finding their own way, everything else
arises from itself. On our tongue, quite silently,
a flowering occurs in error: following this new
spiritual joy come saline images, for a moment
we become human. Running around
in circles is something we understand. Culture
is simply human uninhibitedness.
Joy is as much about tenderness as intoxication with space.
What does a human all have to do in the world. Whoever
believes otherwise can come up with their own answer.

*Um den Preis des Lichts tut die Pflanze alles, was man
von ihr will. Es ist schön, diesen erstaunlichen Vorgang
mit Worten so präzis wie möglich auszudrücken. Wir
sind Pilze, wir haben kein Chlorophyll. Es genügt, wenn
wir nachdenken, um ganze Arbeit zu tun. Der Acker
grenzt an die Welt. Der Garten hat einen Zaun und eine
Türe. Wir kennen also das genaue Maß des Einflusses.
In uns allen ist das Beste die Liebe. Unzertrennlich
sind wir auch schön. Wo man sich nicht mit dem Rand
begnügt, ist das Ausschlaggebende ein Vorhof des
Nichts. Dazu kommt, dass einer nur im Traum sein
Wunschbild liebt. Es ist Honig gleich Honig, Hand die
von unten nach oben darüber hinstreicht. Und doch ist
nicht alles Berechnung. Wie anlehnungsbedürftig
sind wir überzeugt, dass wir keine Sehnsucht haben
nach dem kühlen Gelb der Ährenfelder. Ob er sich
beugt oder aufrichtet, weiß heute jeder, wenn er
krank war. So muss die Entscheidung darüber Kraft
sein, die aus der Erde kommt, es in die Erde zu bringen.*

PAPYRUS

A plant will do anything one requires of it for the
sake of light. Expressing this extraordinary process
as precisely as possible in words is wonderful. We
are mushrooms, we lack chlorophyll. It's enough
that we think, to do a good job. The meadow
borders the world. The garden has a fence and a
gate. So we know the exact extent of influence.
The best in us all is love. Irreducibly we are also
beautiful. Where one is dissatified with the edge
the deciding factor is an antechamber of
nothingness. It follows that only in dreams do you
love your ideal. It's honey like honey, a hand
that caresses upwards. And yet not
everything is calculated. Doesn't our conviction
that we feel no longing for the cool yellow of cornfields
derive from our need for tenderness? Bending or
standing upright, today everyone knows when they
were ill. So the decision about that must be the force,
derived from the earth, to take it into the earth.

*Es war ein weiter Weg von der Steppe bis zur
kompromittierenden Gesellschaft der Obdachlosen.
Jeden Morgen öffnete wildes Unkraut auf dem
Müllhaufen die Augen, von unten nach oben
fiel es ab am Abend. Das Fernweh der Pflanze
ist unser eigenes Jenseits. Kein Dichter kann ihr helfen.
Wirklich? Ist da nicht doch eine der Pflanzenmaterie
innewohnende Sehnsucht, die den am Ort bleibenden
und fortreisenden Menschen wie von der Sonne
geschleuderte Pfeile ins Herz schießt? Nur die
unbegrenzte Größe eines Gottes kommt längst
nicht mehr an. Er schickte einen Mann. Mit der Seele
und mit dem Geist hat er es geschafft, die Verwaltung
des Brotes zu übernehmen. Was ist Unkraut. Eine
unsachgemäße Lieferung? Ein Büro nach dem Vorbild
der architektonischen Eisenbahnorientierung? Was wird
künftig sein. Schlafe, mein Prinzchen, schlaf ein.*

WHAT ARE WEEDS?

It was a long way from the steppe to the
compromising society of the homeless.
Every morning wild weeds open their eyes
to heaps of rubbish, from top to bottom
they mouldered come evening. Plants' wanderlust
is our own beyond. No poet can help them.
Really? Isn't there rather a yearning held
within vegetable material which as if
hurled by the sun fires arrows into the hearts
of those who settle and those who journey on? Though
it's been a while since the limitlessness of a god
arrived. He sent a man. With soul and spirit
he succeeded in taking over the administration
of bread. What are weeds. An
improper delivery? An office modelled on an
architectural preference for railways? What will
the future hold. Sleep now, my prince, go to sleep.

BEREIT SEIN

In der Nacht liege ich und verarbeite Licht. Das Geheimnis,
das unser Leben verlängert, ist das Erinnern. Pflanzen
können es nicht, sie sind Schalen und der freie Wille ist
ein Grundton ihres Wesens. Die Idee alles Wachsenden ist, mit Hilfe
des Lichts Leuna-Werke zu errichten und alle Lücken mit Gewalt
zu schließen. Aufräumen ist ein gutes Wort: Raum aufmachen
und dort aufgeweichte und zerfallende Zellen mit heißen Händen
in Luft und Licht tragen. So bilden sich in Jahrtausenden mächtige
Torflager, die lange Stadien des Austrocknens überwunden haben.
Dann ist das Gerüst entstanden. Es bildet eine eigenartige Folie.
Es ist in seiner Wirkung eng verwandt mit Gedichten. Wie in der
Zusammenarbeit von Gut und Böse schlägt seine Wirkung ins
Gegenteil um, wenn der innere Halt fehlt. Alles liegt in einer Fläche
und nirgends eine Verzweigung, deren Verankerung zu Hilfe käme.
Oben arbeitet die Blätterkrone des Baumes im Lichtbereich. Es ist ein
eigener Gedanke, ganz still zu sein und mit der Welt verklammert.
Jedes einzelne Gras hinter Stacheldraht ist nur scheinbar. Was sonst
noch lebendig heißen mag, hat den Winter zum Freund.

PREPARED

At night I lie down and process light. The secret
which extends our life is memory. Plants
can't do it, they are vessels and free will is
a ground-note of their being. The idea
all growing things share is to construct,
with the help of light, heavy industry and violently
to close all gaps. Clearing is a good word: to clear space
and there to hold with hot hands saturated, decaying cells
in air and light. Thus great reservoirs of peat build up
over millennia, having surmounted long stages of dehydration.
Then the framework is established. It forms a peculiar film
and in its effect is closely related to poems. As with the
interaction of good and evil its effect is inverted
if there is no internal tension. Everything lies on a plane
without ever branching, which would help form an anchor.
Above, the canopy of leaves works in the realm of light. It's a
strange thought, to be quite silent and locked into the world.
Each blade of grass behind barbed wire is only make-believe.
Whatever else might be called alive has winter for a friend.

WANDLUNG

Müllhaufen und Schrottplätze waren von je nahrhaft
genug, die Winter zu überstehen. Denkt man sich
eine Haut darüber, ist es, als ob Kraft in die Erde
hinunter fließt. Das Gefühl unseres Pflanzenursprungs
knüpfen wir an unser erstes Segel. Die Idee von sich
selbst ist den Tieren gleich. Land ist der Begriff, für den
wir zahlen. Es ist uns so fremd geworden, dass wir
leicht eine Grenze erreichen. Dieselbe Fläche, doch
so viele Unterschiede. Das folgsame Gras gehört zu
den Schwachen und umfängt doch den nackt geborenen
Menschen. Selbst Totes, das niemals vom Wind getragen
wurde, wird zu Erde. Wir leben nicht mit eigenem Licht.
Aus dem Schwingen von innen heraus geschieht selten
Erfüllung. Wer andere sucht, sinkt ins unendlich weiche Gras.

MUTABLE

Waste-tips and scrapheaps have always been
rich enough to see the winter out. Imagine
a skin over them and it's like a force flowing
down into the earth. We bind the sense of our
plant origins to our first setting sail. The idea of one's
self is like that of the animals. Land is the concept
we pay for, which has become so alien to us
we soon reach a border. The same expanse, yet
so many differences. Grass is obedient and belongs
with the weak, yet enfolds the naked-born
human. Even dead things which were never wind-
borne turn into earth. We don't live with our own light.
Those swings from inside to out result rarely
in fulfillment. Whoever seeks other people
sinks into endlessly gentle grass.

Die Vorstellung vom Garten des Paradieses
ist auf das Sichtbare gestellt. Das freie Leben
zwang uns in die Schuld. „So sieht man es in der
Natur nicht", sagen wir und wie neue Arme neue
Inseln umfassen, besiedeln Gasfabriken den Rest
der Erde. Die Sonne hat es leicht, das Lichtleben
von oben breitet sich aus bei der Abreise der
Sonnenstrahlen von ihrem Ursprungsort.
Der Schatten kommt vom Leib, anders klingt
das Lichtecho, wo immer ein Mensch nicht
bewohnbar ist. Ein Garten war es! Vom Gras
gibt es überhaupt keinen Abstand mehr. Ich sehe
das Gras und erkenne jetzt, dass ich immer
von Heimweh befallen war. Was wird anders?
Wir werden anders und spüren es nicht.

The idea of the garden of paradise
is based on the visible. A life of freedom
drove us to sin. 'It doesn't look like that
in nature,' we say and, like new arms embracing
new islands, gasworks colonise the rest
of the earth. The sun has it easy, the light-life
from above spreads out as the sun's rays
travel out from their place of origin.
The shadow comes from the body, the light-echo
sounds different wherever a person isn't
habitable. It was a garden! From grass
there's no remove at all any more. I see
the grass and recognise now that I was always
affected by homesickness. What is changing?
We are changing and have no sense of it.

Ich weiß noch genau, wie mich die Welt holte.
Mein Kopf war gequetscht, blau verfärbt, Zangen
zogen an mir. Es gab für mich keine Milch, der Biss
einer Stute hatte die Brust meiner Mutter zerstört.
Ich schlief viel. Und dachte später, dass ich doch
eigentlich Glück gehabt hätte, Blessuren hin oder her.
Was noch geschah? Ich kann leider nicht berichten,
ich weiß es nicht mehr. Mein Säuglingsschlaf dauerte
lang. Ich wünschte mir, endlich zu erwachen. Man
sagt mir, ich hätte bis hin zur Jahrtausendwende
geträumt. Ich empfinde weder Bedauern noch Furcht.
Die alte und die neue Welt ähneln sich. Hier wie dort
fühle ich den Wunsch nach einem Erwachen. Geschichte
ist das, was du erzählt bekommst. Besonders gefallen
mir hier die Blätter an den Bäumen. Es scheint mir, als
wäre damit alles gesagt. Mein Wollen wird kriegerisch.

MIDDLE

I still know exactly how the world fetched me.
My head was squashed, turned blue, and forceps
pulled me. There was no milk for me, a mare's
bite had damaged my mother's breast.
I slept long. And later thought actually
I'd been lucky, give or take the injuries.
What else happened? Unfortunately I can't say,
I no longer know. My suckling-sleep lasted
a long time. I wished and wished I'd wake up. I am
told I could have dreamed until the
millenium. I feel neither fear nor regret.
The old and the new worlds resemble each other. Here
as there I have the wish to awaken. History is
the stories you're told. I especially like
the leaves on the trees here. It seems to me as if
that says everything. My will is becoming martial.

REM

Schau dir gut zu bei Angst um dich:
die kleine schlimme Ewigkeit,
das ist der Augenblick.

Ich wurde in den Wind gesprochen, das Haus
stieß mich aus sich heraus, buchstabierte mich mit
offenen Türen und Fenstern, warf mich hoch,
ich durchbrach die Wolken, schrie AFRIKA und
stieß gegen die Wölbung des höchsten Dachs,
die Barriere aus Luft und Atemlosigkeit. Was folgte
war ein Sturz, ich fiel zurück und donnerte in die
Erde, ich war zum Blitz geworden. Tief in das Innere
führte mich mein Weg, ich veränderte meine Gestalt
und vergaß, wer ich war. Ich dachte nur noch,
dass ich in allem ich war. In allem.

REM

When you're scared have a good look at yourself:
this horrible little eternity
is the blink of an eye.

I was uttered into the wind, the house
thrust me out of itself, spelled me with
open doors and windows, threw me so high
I broke through the clouds, cried AFRICA and
bumped against the dome of the highest ceiling,
the barrier of air and breathlessness. What followed
was a descent, I fell back and thundered into
the earth, I had become lightning. My way
led deep inside, I changed my form
and forgot who I was. I just kept thinking
that in everything I was still I. In everything.

FALB

Eine Nacht herstellen mit
verschütteter Milch den Kreis
füllen begehbare Wände dort
rieselt Laub klappen Bücher
stauben Blumenpressen ein
Schmetterlingsnetz davon

holen Sie sich Alpträume
sehen Sie nach es ist nicht
sicher ob sie alles verstanden

haben wir Felle im Wandschrank
genügend Holz
ein Haus
denken sich die noch nicht
Berührten im Schlaf

DUN

To manufacture a night to
fill with spilt milk the
circle permeable
walls there foliage
rustles books bang shut
flower-presses make dust a
butterfly net's worth

go and fetch nightmares
check as it's not certain
they understood everything

do we have furs in the cupboard
enough wood
a house
think to themselves those not yet
touched in their sleep

TAUCHER

Unter Wasserdecken und im Schlaf
tickt Kellerzählwerk Bläschen hinaus.
Von oben gellende Schreie, geflochtene
Rüstungen, bemalte Helme und Kriegs
Gebrüll. Lange Bambus Fahnen Stangen

in den Gerüsten von Issa. Nicht Stimme
zählt, im tiefen Gang an der Gurgel

vorbei läuft der Atem. Haarbüschel
oder Schnüre gebündelt, von Hand
gefasst: kein Knoten für immer.

DIVER

Below the surface and in sleep
cellar meters tick bubbles out.
Piercing cries from above, woven
armour, painted helmets and war
clamour. Long bamboos, flags, poles

in Issa's scaffolding. It's not voice
that counts, in the gullet's deep channel

breath runs past. Tufts of hair
or braids bound together, grasped
by a hand: no knot's forever.

WIEDERAUFNAHME

Omas Armbanduhr und Papas
Engel zerreißen die Steine im
Kopf. „Tickst du richtig?" schreit
Mama. „Frau Mutter, Sie tun mir
weh". Bibeln werden an diesem Ort
nicht mehr gelesen. Nachts fallen
Wörter wie Messer ins Ohr.

Im Küchenspind steckt ein Geheimnis,
da liegen Matratzen gestapelt, für die
Gefallenen. Mama und Papa und Oma
im Grab. Die Kamera hat dann sehr viel
später ein Mädchen bekommen. Filmriss.

Spazierengehen am Ufer des schönen
Sees. Die große Straße deutet zur Stadt.
Stünden die Fahnen, sähst du den Wind.

Das Gewicht der Steine.

DOUBLE EXPOSURE

Granny's wristwatch and daddy's
angels tear up the stones in
my head. 'Are you still ticking?' shouts
Mummy. 'Dearest mother, you do me
ill.' In this place bibles are
no longer read. At night fall
words like knives into my ear.

A secret hides in the larder,
where matresses lie stacked, for the
fallen. Mummy and daddy and granny
in their graves. Then the camera very much
later had a girl. The film tears.

Walking by the banks of the beautiful
lake. The grand avenue indicates the town.
Were the flags flying, you'd see the wind.

How heavy the stones.

SUCHE

Milchschalen im Regen. Nasser Kaninchenkopf.
Da geht einer durch Wiesen, mit hochgekrempelten
Hosen. Eulenwerg. Nebelbänke. Alles auf Hügeln.
Krähen in niedergedrücktem Gras. Tropfende Tücher.
Ein Blick. Da liegt mein Mund im Schilf. Und dort.
Mein Atem auf dem See. Ein Wellenschlag und bin
nicht ich. Der Ort. Die Dachschindeln. War ein
vergessener Tag. Dort am Rand. Wo die Schwärze
wohnt. Dort im Tal. Am Ende steht das Tor. Hölzerne
Stiefel. Spiegel des Wassers zwischen den Lippen. Still.
Kommt die Flut. Sinken die Steine. Wald in der Hand.
Und ein Schlag. Schlägt das Wort. Weiß der Vogel.
Weiß die Feder. Du. Zitternder Fisch. Schnürender Fuchs.

SEARCH

Bowls of milk in the rain. A rabbit's wet head.
Here's someone walking through meadows with rolled-up
trousers. Owl pellets. Banks of fog. Hillsides.
Crows in flattened grass. Dripping cloths.
A look. Here's my mouth in the reeds. And there.
My breath on the lake. One breaking wave and I'm
no longer I. The place. The roof tiles. The day,
forgotten. There at the edge. Where the darkness
lives. There in the valley. The gate at the end.
Wooden boots, a mirror of water between lips. Silent.
Come the flood, the stones sink. A handful of forest.
And a blow. The impact of a word. White bird,
white feather. You. Quivering fish. Scurrying fox.

MÄRCHENHAFT

Nächtelang durch Wände gehen, die
atmen tiefer noch ein und aus als
einer der stirbt. Heiße Stirnen
drücken Fensterscheiben. Manches
ist wach und dort leckt eine Zunge
den silbernen Löffel Medizin.

Ich gehe, mit dir und dir. Das
Rätseln: Sind wir zwei, oder drei,
oder fünf? So viele Häuser zählt
die Stadt am Morgen. Wie Wale
Fontänen sprühen geht die Sonne
auf und dann die Sterne und

zuletzt der Mond. Alles ist da,
aber den Worten trau nicht.

Auf Halden liegen sie und bleiben
Träume. Und wenn sie nächtens
Flüsse queren, hört man ihre Namen.

BEWITCHING

Walking night after night through
walls which breathe in and out more deeply
than someone dying. Fevered foreheads
press against windowpanes. So much
is awake and a tongue there licks
the silver spoon of medicine.

I walk, with you and you. And
the riddle: how many are we, two,
or three, or five? The house-count's so high
in town in the morning. The way
whales spout fountains the sun
rises and then the stars and

lastly the moon. Everything's there,
but see the words, don't trust them.

They lie in heaps and remain
dreams. And when at night they
cross streams, your hear their names.

HOTZEPLOTZ

Am Morgen, die ganze Mannschaft
versammelt um mein Bett. Fragen:
Ist es zehn, wenn der Vogel kommt?
Lächeln die Pyramiden? Blaue, so
blaue Pflaumen. Und der Leguan?

Milchzahnklappern, Kiebitze, alle. Und
woraus besteht ein Haus? Kennst du
die Wüste? Es geht nach Norden, bis
die Nadel zittert und bricht. Geradeaus,
geradeaus, da ist mein Haus zu Haus.

Nein, ich sags nicht.

Grüner Pfeil und weniger als Knöpfe
am Hemd. Da thront ein König. Sagt:
Rot und Blau ist mir. Geht in die Knie.
Rätsel an der Schnur. Vielleicht, zehn,
ja, zehn. Morgen kommt er wieder.

BOONIES

In the morning, the whole team
gathered round my bed. Questions:
Is it ten when the bird comes?
Do the pyramids smile? Blue, such
blue plums. And the iguana?

Rattling milk-teeth, peewits, the lot. And
what does a house consist of? Have you
been to the desert? In a northerly direction, till
the needle trembles and breaks. Straight ahead,
straight ahead, there's my house, there's my bed.

No, I'm not telling.

A green arrow and even his shirt
lacks buttons. A king, enthroned there, says:
red and blue are mine. Falls to his knees.
The cord's all knotted. Maybe, ten,
yes, ten. He'll be back tomorrow.

NACHTLUFT

Jede Nacht zu Cosimo, der in den Zweigen
lebt. Im Blätterbett ein kleines Gespräch,
bevor der Atem in die Tiefe sinkt. Im Geäst
der Entwurf einer Verfassung für einen
auf den Bäumen gegründeten Idealstaat.

Glühwürmchen und Cosimo mit seiner
Wildkatzenmütze. Erzählt von Rousseau
der mit einer Botanisiertrommel in den
Schweizer Wäldern irrt. Es regnet. Es
donnert. Und im Schein der Blitze tritt
Benjamin Franklin auf die Lichtung:
lässt einen Papierdrachen steigen. Cosimo

träumt. Von Palmen und Wüsten. Von
einem Ballon, der landet im Baum. Er
tritt in die Luft. Sie trägt.

NIGHT AIR

Each night to Cosimo, who lives among
the branches. In the leaf-bed a little dialogue,
till breath sinks to the depths. In the boughs
the draft constitution for a
utopia founded on trees.

Little glow-worms and Cosimo in his
wildcat bonnet. Telling of Rousseau
who wanders the Swiss forests with
a vasculum. It rains. It thunders. And in
a flash of lightning Benjamin
Franklin steps into the clearing, flies
a paper kite higher and higher. Cosimo

dreams. Of palms and deserts. Of
a balloon, which lands in the tree. He steps
into the air. It holds.

ATEMZUG

Entlang den Zäunen wächst Gras. Mein Liebstes
geht über die Hügel, mein Licht wächst im Baum
so hell dass jeder Vogel Komet ist. Wind weht
und streicht die Häuser blau. Mein Liebstes ist eine
verlorene Feder, ein abgebrochener Stern, es
ist die nächste Haltestelle und von allen Zügen
der Langsamste. Von Halt zu Halt ziehe ich
Stöcke aus den Händen der Schrankenwärter als
wäre mein Weg eine Straße von brennenden Gleisen.

BREATH

Grass grows by the fences. My dearest
is crossing the hills, in the tree my light grows
so bright each bird is a comet. The breeze
paints the houses blue. My dearest is a
missing feather, a snapped-off star, is
the next station and of all trains the very
slowest. From stop to stop I pull
the signalling-discs from the gate-keepers' hands
as if my path were a street of burning rails.

PATIENCE

Die Halbtiefen, so sprach er
von den Schwellenängsten, trat
Zimmertüren ein und brüllte von
Vergeblichkeit. Es waren harte Tage.
Bemannte Raumschiffe verschlimmerten
die Lage. Der König lag im Koma. Das
Flüstern der Astronomen verlor sich im
Wind, der die Buchseiten aufschlug.
Neue Muster sollten entworfen werden
für die geschlossenen Webereien. All dies
wurde geträumt in der Nacht zum Freitag.
Das letzte Schaf verließ gerade den Raum.
Die Morgenzeitung ungewöhnlich offen:
Aller sieben todsünden schönste:
Der blutrötliche psalter, den uns
Ein ferner irrer traum schlägt.

PATIENCE

The half-depths, that was how he spoke
of his fear of thresholds, kicked
in doors and bawled about futility.
They were difficult days. Manned
spacecraft made the situation
worse. The king was in a coma. The
wind took the astronomers' whispers
and blew open the pages of a book.
New designs were to be drawn up
for the abandoned weaving-mills. All this
was dreamt in the night of Thursday to Friday.
The last sheep was just leaving the room.
Unusually frank, the morning paper:
Of all seven deadly sins the sweetest:
The blood-reddish psalter, with which
A strange, faraway dream smites us.

BAHAMUT

Ich bin der Fisch, der zum Luftholen
die Oberfläche des Wassers küsst:
du siehst die Berührung, die Kreise
die sie zieht, aber mich, den Fisch
siehst du nicht. Und meine Lippen
machen Wellen, die über das Wasser
an die Ufer der Meere eilen. Ich bin es.
Mit allem, was ich dir nicht sagen kann.
Hast du je einen wie mich sprechen hören?
Der Regen spielt mit mir. Meine Welt
hält mich. Ich bin der Fisch.

BAHAMUT

I am the fish who, coming for air
kisses the water's surface:
you see the disturbance, the
circles it creates, but me, the fish,
you don't see. And my lips make
waves which race across the water to
the shores of all the seas. That is me.
With everything I cannot say to you.
Have you ever heard speak one such as I?
The rain plays with me. My world
sustains me. I am the fish.

ZUNGE. SÄNFTE.

Ich kannte diesen Teil des Landes
nicht. Man schickte mir einen Brief
und bat um mein Kommen. Ich komme
rief ich, mein Gepäck verlor ich noch vor
der Abfahrt, auch das Buch, ein
Geschenk und die Karte mit Grüßen meiner Stadt:
eating strawberries in the necropolis. *Eile*
sprach mein Gedächtnis, der Weg, du erinnerst
ihn? Ich musste schlafen, schlief ein auf
der Reise, im Schlaf träumte ich, im Schlaf
fand ich Blumen und dachte an ein Mitbringsel:
das ist üblich in der Fremde. Träumte
von der Ankunft, man reichte mir Schalen
the flesh was tender, red as cactusflower
mit leeren Händen und schlafend
trug man mich über die Grenze.

TONGUE. SEDAN.

I didn't know this corner of
the country. I was sent a letter
asking me to come. I'm coming,
I cried, and lost my luggage before I'd
even set out, including the book, a
present and the card with greetings from my town:
eating strawberries in the necropolis. Haste
urged memory, which way, can you
remember? I had to sleep, slept
on the journey, in my sleep I dreamed that
in my sleep I found flowers and thought
of bringing a little something:
that's usual abroad. Dreamed that,
arriving, I was handed bowls
the flesh was tender, red as cactusflower
empty-handed and sound asleep
I was carried over the border.

DRONTE

Hörte in der Nacht ein Wesen schreien, draußen
vor dem Fenster: „Ich brauche einen Gefährten!"
heulte es, im Mondlicht stehend, verkümmertes
Gefieder, groß wie ein Meeräffchen, nur klettern
konnte es nicht. Die Flügel stummlig, Flaumläppchen.
Wackelt mit coupiertem Schwanz, kommt wieder. Jede
Nacht Gebrüll: „Ich brauche einen…". Ist ja gut. Komm
her du Tier. Will dich ein wenig drücken und zupfen an
deiner Gänsehaut. Und überhaupt: nimm doch mich. Wir
gehen auf Reisen und schreiben uns die schönsten Briefe:
„Werter Apterygier, cher Didu, hier auf den Molukken ist's
so einsam, ohne Sie". Und du: „Ich raste im Schatten des
Kalvarienbaums und knacke Nüsse. Ihr Dodo de Nausée". Vier
von deiner Art als Mahlzeit für hundert Matrosen, heiliger Nazar,
mein König von der Schwaneninsel, oiseau lyre, lustig war die Jagd
auf dich und einfach. Nicht mal ein Häuflein Asche übrig. Lass uns
ein wenig schlafen. Und träumen. Es war einmal. Im blauen Ozean.

DODO

Heard at night a creature cry, outside
the window: 'I need a companion!',
it howled, by the light of the moon, shabby
plumage, big as a guenon, not that it could
climb. Stumpy wings, like fluffy cloths.
Waddles with its undulating tail, returns. Each
night a commotion: 'I need a…'. OK, OK. Come
here, beast. I want to give your goose-flesh a stroke
and a squeeze. And anyhow: choose me. We'll
travel and write each other the sweetest letters:
'Worthy Apterygian, dear Didu, here in the Moluccas without
you it's so lonely.' And you: 'I'm resting in the shade of
the tambalacoque, cracking nuts. Your Dodo de nausée.' Four
of your kind enough to feed a hundred sailors, blessed Nazarite,
my king of Swan Island, oiseau lyre, hunting you was delightful
and so easy. Not even a pile of ashes left. Let's sleep
a while. And dream. Once upon a time. The ocean blue.

ROTUNDE

Dein warmer Handschlag lässt mich knien
vor den Heiligen der Raststätten und
Autobahnzubringer, der U-Bahn-Schächte
und Ramschläden. Gleichzeitig hefte ich
mehrsprachige Orden ans Revers: so
stützen wir uns als Heldinnen der Fremde
verschicken Pläne für strategisches Denken
im Traum. Von wegen Steine, in den
ausgebeulten Jackentaschen kauern
Sternzeichentiere und bergen deine Fäuste
wenn sie zerkratzt und schreiend das Dunkel
suchen. Morgen gehst du wieder los, in die
Kreisrundstraße, wo die Kessel der Söldner
auf dem Feuer stehen und gesottenes
Herz als Delikatesse geboten wird.

ROTUNDA

Your warm handshake has me kneeling
to the saints of motorway slip-roads and
service-stations, of the Underground's shafts
and junk-shops. At the same time I pin
to my lapel decorations in various tongues: thus
we back up our claim to be heroines from abroad
further plans for strategic thinking
in dreams. Never mind stones, in the
jacket's bulging pockets cower
the creatures of the zodiac and your fists
hide when scratched and screaming they long
for darkness. Tomorrow you set out again,
for the ring-road, where the solderers'
kettles sit on fires and boiled
heart is offered as a delicacy.

VON STEINEN BESCHÜTZT

Unter Eid spreche ich zu mir: es ist sinnlos
diese Anhäufung von Gut, also weg damit
und alle Pachtverträge aufgelöst. Nicht
Halt machen vor dem Rest, ein Obdach
beziehen in der Luft, den Grund verfeuern
es ist Herbst, der Boden will Asche.
In sich gekehrt wird alles zur Nahrung
für bewachte Brandstätten.

PROTECTED BY STONES

Under oath I say to myself, this accumulation
of goods makes no sense, so
out with the lot, and cancel all the leases.
Don't stop there, pitch camp
in the air and torch the ground,
it's autumn and the earth wants ashes.
Everything turned in on itself becomes fuel
for orderly bonfires.

LANDMARKEN

*Der mir Fremde stürzte unmittelbar vor meinen Füßen
zu Boden, schlug mit dem Kopf auf. Sein Hund lief weit
entfernt auf einem Acker. Ich stand und betrachtete
Schlehen tragende Zweige. Mein Fall war mir bekannt.
Erste Hilfe bedeutet: Steine anheben, der Grenzstein
von weitem war auch nicht größer als die Splitter
an seiner Schläfe, im versickernden Blut. Das Haupt
lag schwer im Arm, als der Blick wiederkehrte. Mein
Fremdsein war einen Lidschlag lang nah, dann war ich
ein Tier, wurde der Hund, der seinem Menschen wieder
auf die Beine half. Wir entfernten uns mit den Steinen.*

LANDMARKS

A stranger to me he crashed to the ground right
at my feet, hitting his head. His dog was running
in a distant meadow. I stood and observed
sloe-bearing branches. What befell was familiar to me.
First aid means: raising stones, the boundary-stone
in the distance was itself no larger than the gash
on his temple, seeping blood. His head
was lying heavily on my arm, when sight returned. My
estrangement blinked into close-up, then I was
an animal, became the dog, which helped his master
back to his feet. We departed with the stones.

ÜBERFÜHRUNG

Sonntags über den Fluss gehen, über die Spree
am Schiffbauerdamm. Schwarzer Tunnel,
dunkel, eisern, vergitterter Körper
unter dem es fließt. Kein Laut von den
Zungen des Wassers, die lecken die Pfeiler
grau. Im Innern hat sich die Nacht vor dem
Morgen versteckt und hustet. Absatzklappern.
Flirrendes Echo der Züge, die Brücke wiegt
Platten aus Teer in den Schlaf. Auf steinernen
Stufen liegt ein Gott und lächelt im Traum.

CHECKPOINT

Crossing the river on a Sunday, the Spree
at Schiffbauerdamm. A black tunnel,
darkness and iron, a creature of mesh and grilles
above the flow – soundless
tongues of water licking the piers
grey. Inside, night has hidden from morning
and wheezes. A clatter of heels, an echoey
whirr of trains, the bridge is rocking
slabs of tar asleep. On stone steps
a god lies, smiling in his dreams.

Grauer Stein ohne Wald.
Der Gärtner darf darin
nicht graben.

Grauer Stein: ein Bild von uns.

Du schläfst schlecht, spürst
das Wachsein, das Schlafen
in den Augen anderer.

Ich glaube schon, dass es
dieses Tier, das wir gewusst
nicht ruhen lässt.

Werde ich mich entwirren?
Dass ich gerade das nicht weiß
in Zusammenhang mit mir
das ist komisch und schön.

Erinnerst du dich?
Erinnere mich gut, oh ja:

Das Amazonasgebiet
aus den Augen verlieren
sähe nach Tränen aus.

Grey stone without forest.
The gardener may
not dig there.

Grey stone: a reflection of us.

You sleep badly, sense
the wakefulness and sleep
in others' eyes.

I really think it can't
leave the animal we knew
in peace.

Will I unknot myself?
That it's this – this –
I don't know about myself
is weirdly lovely.

Do you remember?
Oh, I remember all right:

To lose sight of
the Amazon region
would look like tears.

Zeit, die keine Bedrohung darstellt:
meine sieben Jahre im Finstern
unter der Berührung des Lichts.

Und die Reinen
Tätowierten: geliebte schlafende
Tiefe und dahinter im Blut das nackte Wort.

Angst vor bestimmter und klarer Wahrheit
wie aus der Asche ein Stamm wird.

Aufbrechen will ich, zu sehen
die flügellos steinernen Engel
wie sie sich insgeheim lieben

und sind gefallen nackt auf das Erdreich
wie Kiesel

alle existieren
doch nur wir selber sind.

Time, which doesn't represent a threat:
my seven years among the shades
touched by light.

The Pure
and Tattooed: beloved sleeping
depths and behind in the blood the naked word.

Fear of unqualified transparent truth
as from the ashes a stem grows.

I want to set out to see
the wingless stone angels
how they secretly love each other

and have fallen naked to earth
like pebbles

everything exists
but only we ourselves are.

BAUEN IM HOCHGEBIRGE

In der unwahrscheinlichsten der Städte verband sich
Regenwasser mit dem Gewölbe des Mondlichts. Die
Vorstellung von den Pyramiden verwirklichte sich in
Glasblöcken. Der König starb in der Blütezeit des Reichs
und während sein Leichnam erstarrte, verstummte der Chor.
Denn es war gar nicht daran gedacht, Musik wieder erstehen
zu lassen. Ein Erdbeben ließ Gestirne ins Meer stürzen,
Eisenkristalle verbanden sich bruchlos mit Feuerschlünden.
An einem Fenster beleuchteten neun silberne Glühbirnen
diese Inschrift: „Denn was ihr vergeblich sucht, ist das Wunder".
Man fühlt es bei längst niedergegangener Sonne, deren
versunkene Massen beigesetzt werden in strömendem Regen,
um die Gestalt der Flammen, die man nicht sieht, zu vergolden.

BUILDING AT ALTITUDE

In the most improbable of cities rainwater
bonded with the dome of moonlight. The
idea of the pyramids was realised in glass
bricks. The king died at the empire's zenith
and as his corpse stiffened, the choir fell silent.
For the last thing on anyone's mind was the revival
of music. An earthquake tumbled stars into the sea,
iron crystals bonded seamlessly with gulfs of fire.
At a window nine silver lightbulbs illuminated
the inscription, 'For what ye seek in vain is miracles'.
You feel this long after the sun has set, its
sunken masses buried in pouring rain,
so the body of flames, unseen, turns golden.

GLÄSERN

*Im Traum sah ich eine seltsame Stadt. Ich trug sie
auf meinen Schultern. Man konnte dort nicht leben
sie war gebaut aus Eisen und Luft, schlechter Luft
wie aus Kanälen. Gerümpel, Sperriges und ich
der Fluss, den diese Stadt staute. Sie ragte tief
in mich hinein, so tief, dass ihre Keller mein Herz
ummauerten. Weiter nichts.*

GLASSY

Dreaming, I saw a strange city. I carried it
on my shoulders. No one could live there
it was made of iron and air, bad air
like that from ditches. Junk, hulks and I
the river this city dammed. It reached
so deep inside me its cellars had walled in
my heart. That's all.

Zwischen Fellbesteigung und Marderloch
graben wir knurrend die gebleckten Zähne
uns ins Fleisch. Drüben schiebt eine Rakete
sich in den Mond, aufgerissene Häute hängen
seitwärts zu Boden, wir sagen nichts und
tun so als sähen wir und verstünden ohne
Worte. Im Schlaf hören wir die Trommeln.

Du läufst los. Ich folge nicht, ich gehe.
Auch wenn der Mond scheint und die Raben
krächzen, heiser und verzweifelt, all dies bringt
den Stein nicht mehr zurück, den, der ins Rollen
kam. Es ist nur noch Zeit für den Schlaf.

Wir hören nicht auf zu lieben. Wir sehen
Knochen und Laub und die Zeit schlüpft in
die Rolle der Siegerin. Mit verschlagenem Atem
führen wir schwere Zungen aus im Gelände.
Dann legst du noch einmal – nur noch ein
einziges Mal – mir die Hand auf die Brust. Wir
lieben immer und stochern nach Resten in uns.

FIFTY WAYS

Between hidebound mounting and the marten's burrow
we snarl and dig our bared teeth into each
other's flesh. Above, a rocket is thrusting
into the moon, torn skins hang
sideways to the floor, we say nothing and
make out we can see and understand without
words. In our sleep we hear the drums.

You run off. I don't follow, I leave.
Even when the moon shines and crows
caw, hoarse and wretched, none of this
brings back the stone which is already
rolling. There's only time for sleep.

We don't stop loving. We see
bones and leaves and time slips into
the role of Victory. Our breath taken away
we exercise heavy tongues in open country.
Then once more – one very last time – you place
your hand on my breast. We go on
loving and pick at the remnants inside us.

STELLARIA

Unnütze Gebete, nichts kommt im Schlaf
über dich. Du reinigst Metall, Körbe voll
von fremdartigen Formen, die du nicht
zusammenbringen kannst. Welche
Maschine, wenn du wüsstest, welcher
Apparat? Eine Flinte könnte es sein,
oder ein Sternfernrohr. Das Tuch voll
von schwarzen Flecken, heut Nacht
werden Himmelskörper abgeschossen.

Useless prayers, when you sleep nothing
threatens you. You polish metal, basketfuls
of the weirdest bits and pieces you can't
fit together. Which mechanism,
if you had the know-how, which
machine? It could be a rifle
or an astronomical telescope. Black
smudges all over the cloth, tonight
heavenly bodies, fired upon, will fall.

TACITURNO

Für gewöhnlich stehen die Türen
der Tragödie offen. Amseln, still
wie in einem Gemälde, fangen an
zu schlagen, wie die Turmuhr
um Mitternacht, ein plötzlicher
Wind, der aufschreckt, das Rasche.

Wenn also etwas plötzlich ins Auge
schießt, die Träne, das Staubkorn,
auf impressionistische Weise
verschwommen die Zweige im Laub
Spalier stehen, erwartungsvoll, ist
nichts gewonnen. Schweig lieber.

Es geht um nicht viel mehr als
um Glas, um Sand und um das Rätsel,
was beides mit deinem Auge macht.

TACITURN

As a rule the doors of tragedy
stand open. Blackbirds, as silent
as a painting, start to
trill, like the church clock
sounding at midnight, a sudden
wind, terrible and swift.

So if something suddenly
shoots into your eye – tears,
a speck of dust – and,
impressionistically blurred,
the branches in the leaves form
an expectant guard of honour,
nothing is gained. Best keep quiet.

It's about not much more
than glass, sand, and the riddle
of what the two of them do to your eye.

ALBA

An den Anlegestellen schwappt Wasser über
unseren Atem, während wir ankern, uns ansehen:
wie alt wir sind, in Gedanken und in den Namen,
die anderes sagen: gestrandeter Wal, der Albatros,
du ahnst, dies hat die Arrhythmie des Herzschlags
ausgelöst. Doch, Alba, wenn alle Handlang
Graupel in dein Aug schlägt, wirst du fraglos wach
sein, wie im Traum. Vieles klingt nach, wandelt
die halben Sachen in Raum, wo man wahr sagt,
ganz am Anfang. Ist nicht diese Angewohnheit
alles zu verlieren, das augenscheinlichste
Zeichen. Wie ausdauernd wir nur warten, ohne
Erwartung zu sein, ohne Atem, Haut, Alba.

ALBA

At the berths, water spills over our breath
as we drop anchor, and look at each other:
how old we are, in thought and in the names
which mean something else: beached whale, the albatross,
you think this might have triggered the irregular
heartbeat. Still, Alba, if all this repetition
shoots hailstones into your eyes, you'll be unquestioningly
awake, as in dreams. Much resonates, shifts
the half-formed things in space where it's all foretold,
right at the start. Isn't this habit of losing everything
the clearest sign. How long we wait, simply to be
without expectation, without breath, skin, Alba.

KÖNNEN

Eine Kunst: die Klarheit des Wassers im tiefen
Becken bis zum Kiesel am Grund. Das Knistern
im dunklen Korb: Skorpion oder Käfer? Streck
die Hand aus, kennst du es nicht? Ich kann die
Kühle schmecken, den öligen Kern, kindliche Küsse,
die Lakonie des Abends: eingekerbt in die Karte
Makedoniens, wo Krieger Tabak spucken und
Tage zerkauen. Diese kleine Kunst, ein gekrümmtes
Haar aufzurichten, kaputte Zäune, geknicktes Gras.

CAPABLE

An art: clarity of water in a deep basin right
to the gravel at the bottom. The rustling
in the basket's gloom: scorpion or beetle? Reach
out your hand, don't you know? I taste
coolness, the oily kernel, a childish kiss,
laconic evenings: notched into the map of
Macedonia, where warriors spit tobacco and
chew days. This minor art, of righting a
frazzled hair, broken fences, crushed grass.

ORGANISCH

Hör zu, das große Orakel weht Brisen von
Ocker ins Ohr: mein Trost, und du, Vogel,
der ein Omen aus dem Schnabel verlor.
Wort, im Boden vertäut, gelogen. Ein
Segler, von Lotsen gezogen, trägt Flor.
Amazonasgebiet, kein Ort, eine Losung
nur, wie der gordische Knoten. Nachts
stoßen Boote ins Delta vor, ins Geflecht
der Aorta, in die Landschaft Moor.

ORGANIC

Can you hear, the holy oracle is blowing airs from
ochre into the ear: consoling me, as you do, bird,
who lost an omen from your beak.
Word, fast in the floor, sham. A
sailor, towed by pilots, wearing crape.
Amazonas, not a place, just a
code, like the Gordian knot. At night
boats broach the delta, the aorta's
network and the landscape moor.

NEGATIV

Das Weiß in Fetzen gefunden, so zerrissen wie
die Arbeit von Monaten bisweilen vergeblich scheint.
Und die Plakate an den Wänden: ich vermisse, ich
vermisse.... Mein Gedächtnis ist eine Dunkelkammer
die nur blutrotem Licht Einlass gewährt.

NEGATIVE

White, found in ragged shreds, just as
sometimes months of work seem futile.
The posters on the walls – I've lost, I'm
missing.... My memory is a darkroom
into which only blood-red light is admitted.

NODUM

Ungestillt – der Fortgang einiger Rufe, die
mich erreichten, durchstießen und sich
verfingen. Unentwirrt die Flüstersprache:
Ich weiß, wovon sie spricht, aber was?
Zähe Handreichungen, Strichversuche, das

was bleibt

bleibt geöffnet, ein Ja, erstickt. Kehllaute,
Röntgenfilme: a, b, c – tongue movement.

NODUS

Unrelieved – the progress of certain calls, which
reached me, broke through and then
caught. The tangled language of whispers:
I know that of which it speaks, but what?
Awkward helping-hands, attempted strokes, that

which remains

remains open, a yes, stifled. Guttural sounds,
X-ray films: a, b, c – tongue movement.

AB MORGEN WIRD ALLES ANDERS

Am heutigen Tag, morgens, von neuem
begonnen, das Kapital zu prüfen,
fallende Münzen zu fangen,
im Hasch-mich-Spiel
um Leben und Tod
der Wörter, des Vermögens
alles in fiktive Währung zu tauschen.

FROM TOMORROW IT'LL ALL BE DIFFERENT

Today, in the morning, starting
from scratch, to examine capital,
to catch falling coins,
to change,
in the game of Mousetrap
that's life or death
for words, for fortunes,
everything into made-up currency.

ÜBERGANG

Der Zug überquerte den Fluss
und seine Adern. Felder zogen vorüber
Steine leuchteten in den Rillen.
Schotter der Weg, auf dem wir fuhren.
Verlässliche Stromleitungen, verirrte
Zeilen der Luft. Bäume legten Früchte
wie gefallene Blätter ins Gras. Der Zug
fuhr verspätet aufs Land.

Die Ankunft, ungewiss bis zuletzt
verkündeten Vögel, die der Wind
gegen die Scheiben warf.

CROSSING

The train crossed the river
and its arteries. Fields marched past
stones gleamed in the furrows.
Gravel, the path we were travelling.
Reliable power supply, straying
lines in the sky. Trees dropped fruit
like falling leaves into the grass. The train
moved through the countryside behind schedule.

The arrival, uncertain till the end
was announced by birds the wind
threw against the windows.

ZÜNDSCHNUR

Wie diese Nebelfeuchte drückt, die nicht ganz zu Eis verklumpten
kaltgepressten Harztropfen feiner Nadelgehölze, stickiger Dunst
schwelender Komposthügel, flügellahme Amseln, mein geheimer
Kohlenkeller, Vorratskammer schwarzer Partikel, gefrorener
Kristalle, Einwecksalamander, mein Vogelscheuchenhut
des Sommers, schimmelnde Koffer und die bald glimmenden
Späne, knackende Hölzer und Brünste unterirdischer Feuer
meine brennenden, Schnee fressenden Hände.

SAFETY FUSE

How this damp air presses, the drops of resin from
conifer twigs the cold hasn't quite congealed, cloying vapours
from smouldering compost-heaps, broken-winged blackbirds, my secret
coal cellar, store cupboard of black particles and frozen
crystals, a bottled salamander, my summer scarecrow
hat, mouldering cases and planks about to glow, crackling
pieces of wood and the lusts of underground fires
my burning, snow-guzzling hands.

PARFAIT

Grasnarben unter Schnee versteckt
von Wind und Winter zugedeckt
stäubt Weite einen fernen Blick
kehrt keine Wolke mehr zurück

~

Das Schneetellerchen bis zum Rand gefüllt und
Hyazinthen mit Sand bedeckt, mit warmer Hand
die Fenster berührt und Glas gesprochen, die
Wäscheleine hat im Regen ihre Farbe verloren.

~

Im Winterkleid den Weg entlang, der streckenweise
Frühling spielt, ein Dress mit Mustern. Trompetenchöre
jauchzend in Wehen gesunken, metallischer Geschmack
von Schnee, Mundstücke an Lippen gefroren.

~

meine ungeteilte art dir mitzuteilen, dass ich
eine glaswand bin, neuerdings, und keinesfalls
mir fremde schuhe tragen werde. dass ich
höflich bin und auch die tiere gut behandle.
was ich jeden tag zerschlage, will ich dich
nicht wissen lassen. du könntest annehmen
ich hielte dich für einen spiegel.

PARFAIT

The sward is hidden under snow
above, the winds of winter blow
when wide expanses gaze beyond
no cloud will ever come again
~
The saucer full to the brim with snow and
hyacinths covered with sand, with a warm hand
touching the window and speaking glass, the
washing line has lost its colour in the rain.
~
In winter dress along the path, which seems to play
at spring in parts, an outfit made to a pattern. Jubilant
trumpet bands sunk in gloom, metallic taste
of snow, lips frozen to mouthpieces.
~
my impartial way of imparting to you that i
am of late a wall of glass and under no
circumstances will wear shoes not my own. that i
am polite and also kind to animals.
what i obliterate each day i don't want
you to know. you might assume
i took you for a mirror.

OBSTFLIEGEN ÜBER DER SCHALE

Wär so ein schöner Sommertag, mit auffliegenden
Admiralen aus den Schmetterlingsbüschen in Nachbars
Garten, während Flüssigkeiten an Mülltonnenrändern
eindicken zu harzigen Tropfen, wie Sirup an der Luft,
klebrig und zäh. Ich möchte sofort... aber ich kann nicht.
Muss weiterhin mit schweren Lidern aus dem Fenster
sehen und Fliegen totschlagen. Der Wind weht den
süßlichen Zersetzungsgestank organischen Abfalls
irgendwohin. Die Presslufthammerbataillone der
Stadtwerke rücken näher. Genau: das Geläute
der Klangstäbe? Sonst bei jedem Hauch so
chinesisch, als säße man in einer Pagode
und läse Lao Tse, während ein flinkfüßiger
Diener daran dächte, das Plätschern der
Zeit mit feinem Pinsel zu kalligraphieren.

FRUIT-FLIES ABOVE THE BOWL

It would have been such a nice summer's day, admirals
flying up from the buddleia in the neighbour's
garden, while liquids on the rims of dustbins
coagulate in resinous drops, like syrup in the air,
sticky and glutinous. Right now I'd like to… but I can't.
I have to go on looking out of the window with heavy
eyelids and killing flies. The breeze wafts the
cloying scent of decomposing organic waste
somewhere. The municipal department of works'
battalions of pneumatic hammers draw nearer. Exactly:
the sound of claves? Otherwise each breath of wind
seems oriental, as if one were sitting in a pagoda
reading Lao-Tsu, while a nimble servant with
a fine brush has thought to calligraph
the way time laps and splashes.

DER GARTEN VON E

Wake, butterfly –
it's late, we've miles
to go together.

Viele, unzählige Meilen Worte fern
liegt der Garten von E, am östlichen
Rand der Milchstraße. Meister Basilius
berichtet davon und zeigt in den
Ordnungen des Herbstes Früchte,
die der Garten schenkt: eine Wunderblume,
Jasminum Indicum, den Pfefferstrauch,
die Rose von Jericho, umgeben
von Balsamapfel und Balsamine. Mitten
im Grün die Steineiche, sie beschirmt
mit ihrem Blattwerk jenen, dessen Name
verstreut ist in alle Winde, der in Licht
ertrank, in ihrem Schatten sitzend. Die
Gärtner gehen ihrem Tagwerk nach, in der
Nacht deuten sie auf den Mond. Ein
Schmetterling durchgaukelt die Luft,
hält an auf einer Blüte, die ihn nicht rief.
Im Dunkel des Raums ist nichts, worin
der Garten ruht. Genannt wär es dahin
und muss vergessen sein. Alles blüht und
vergeht und kommt wieder. Erinnere dich.

THE GARDEN OF E

Wake, butterfly —
it's late, we've miles
to go together.

Numerous, innumerable miles and words away
lies the Garden of E, at the eastern
edge of the Milky Way. Master Basilius
writes of it and shows in their proper
order autumn's fruits which
the garden brings forth: a four o'clock,
Jasminum Indicum, the pepper vine,
the rose of Jericho, surrounded
by balsam apple and balsam. Amidst
the green the holm oak's canopy
shelters the one whose name is
scattered to the winds, who drowned
in light, sitting in its shadow. The
gardeners undertake their daily tasks, at
night they point to the moon. A
butterfly flutters through the air,
lands on a bloom which did not call it.
In the darkness of space there's nothing
in which the garden lies. Named, it would be over
and must be forgotten. Everything blooms and
withers and recurs. Remember this.

Bald soll Frühling sein und dass ich es
ahne, zerrt an mir wie die Brise, die
heranweht, ihre Klauen in Fleisch
schlägt, diese blasse, lichtscheue Haut
aufreißt, damit Wunden sich schließen
und etwas wieder heilen kann.

Spring's due soon and, so I
sense it, tugs me like the breeze that
blows this way, claws piercing
flesh and tearing this pale skin un-
used to light, so wounds can close
and something starts to heal again.

ABFLUG

Im Frühling war es soweit, da wurde
mein Bündel auf die Straße geworfen:
und nun sieh selbst, wie du die Lieder
der Schwalben begreifst. Diese Vögel
sind schnell, gewiss, aber das war es nicht
was mich so begriffsstutzig machte. Meine
Familie sammelte Nester, ein alter und
ehrwürdiger Beruf. Mein Onkel schlug mir
auf den Mund, als er mich erwischte
beim Wärmen der Eier. Der Himmel
über den Häusern schien durchkreuzt von
Pfeilen und Krallen, spitzen Schnäbeln.
Die verdammten Wetterhähne konnten
auch nicht mehr als rostig klappern.
Und mir gelingt nur eins: tote Vögel
aus Pfützen zu bergen im Herbst, wenn
sie auf der Flucht verloren gehen.

In spring it had reached the stage that
my pack was thrown onto the street:
now see for yourself what sense you can
make of the swallows' songs. These birds
are certainly fast, but that wasn't what
made me so slow-witted. My
family gathered nests, an old and
honourable profession. My uncle punched
me in the mouth when he caught me
keeping eggs warm. The sky
above the houses seemed crisscrossed
with darts and claws, pointed beaks.
The damnable weathercocks too by then
were rusty and could do no more than rattle.
And I succeed only in this: retrieving
dead birds from puddles in autumn when
during their flight they lose their way.

BIS ZU ALLEN DEINEN ENDEN

Zum Bett der Sommer trug die liebste Nacht:
Nur schlaflos sein, nur liebhaben
Ich gewann dich so lieb
gewann dich so lieb
Ein Herz ist in das Herz der Nacht geschlüpft
es kann nicht schlafen
kann nicht schlafen

schleicht hinter die Rippen der Nacht
schwingendes Herz
welches weiter schlägt
um dein Gesicht und mein Gesicht

Du bist so ganz
bis zu allen deinen Enden
mit Wolkenzügen in Wind getaucht
singt der Fremdling aus den Flammen

Ich hatte ein kleines Erinnern
aus den Trümmern geborgen
und die alten Namen verbrannt

TO YOUR EACH AND EVERY LIMIT

Summer took to bed the sweetest night:
to be sleepless, to be fond
I grew so fond of you
so fond of you
A heart has slipped into the heart of night
it can't sleep
can't sleep

steals beneath the ribs of night
swinging heart
which goes on beating
around your face around my face

You are complete
to your each and every limit
with cloud-features dipped in wind
sings the stranger from the flames

I'd borrowed from the rubble
a little memory
and burned the old names

Stille. Weiße See.
Die hängenden Gärten
des Herbstes. Fallendes
Grün. Oben fliegen
die Wolken. Niemals
trank ein Vogel
Muttermilch. Ich
bleibe am Herd.
Die Vögel reisen.

Silence. The white sea.
The hanging gardens
of autumn. Falling
green. Overhead
clouds fly. Never
did a bird drink
breast milk. I
stand at the stove.
The birds depart.

Das ist derselbe Weg, dieselbe Spur
und der Fluss… man könnte sagen,
er bewegt sich wie immer, sogar der
Vogelschwarm taucht auf wie verabredet
über dieser Stellung von Bäumen, die verlässlich
Laub lassen und wiederkehren. Immer bin ich es,
die in diesem Feld steht und Koordinaten prüft;
nie vergeht die Zeit dazwischen anders als immerzu
jetzt: die Luft, zerteilt. Ich halte mich, so gut es mir
eben gelingt, an diesen Aussichtspunkt, der mir unter
der Erde nicht anders scheint, als von diesem Ort aus:
Stein unter Wasser. Etwas könnte darüber hinaus führen,
in die Stadt, in ein Land, verdrehte Straßenschilder, oder
auf den Stein, dieses Blatt, ein Meer? Ich glaube diesem
Gedächtnis schon lange nicht mehr, dass es zu mir gehört.

TERRESTRE

This is the same path, the same trail
and the river… it might be said
it moves as it always does, indeed the
flock of birds appears as if on cue
above this stand of trees, which reliably
lose leaves and recur. It's always me
in the field here checking co-ordinates;
the time in between never passes other than as
always now; the air, shredded. I stick, as well as I can,
to this vantage point, which seems to me no different
under the earth than from this place:
stone under water. Something might lead out above it,
to the town, to a country, road-signs switched round, or
onto the stone, this leaf, a sea? It's been a while
since I believed this memory was even mine.

NACHTLUFT / NIGHT AIR Cosimo is the main character in
the novel *The Baron in the Trees* by Italo Calvino.

PATIENCE In German 'Patience' refers to the card game. The
last three lines are from 'Sieben fantasmagorische grueguerías'
('Seven phantasmorgorical grueguerias') by H.C. Artmann.

BAHAMUT 'Bahamut' is a huge fish in Arabian mythology,
cf 'behemoth'. See *Arabian Nights*, Night 496; and Borges, *Book
of Imaginary Beings*.

ZUNGE. SÄNFTE. / TONGUE. SEDAN. The English lines in
the German original are from Michael Hulse's poem 'Eating
Strawberries in the Necropolis'.

ALBA 'Alba' – meaning 'dawn' in Italian – is a word used by
Paul Celan in the poem 'Es ist alles anders' ('Everything is
different').

THE GARDEN OF E The epigraph is a haiku by Matsuo Bashō,
translated by Lucien Stryk. 'Basilius' refers to Basilius Besler,
who compiled the florilegium *Hortus Eystettensis* (*The Garden of
Eichstätt*) of 1613.

ACKNOWLEDGEMENTS

Some of the German originals have appeared in the following publications: *Days of Poetry and Wine* (Medana, Slovenia); *Jahrbuch der Lyrik 2013* (Deutsche Verlags-Anstalt); *Jahrbuch der Lyrik 2017 (Schöffling & Co.)*; *Konzepte. Zeitschrift für Literatur*; *Literatur in Bayern*; *manuskripte*; *neue deutsche literatur 2/04* (Aufbau-Verlag).

Some of the English translations have appeared in the anthologies *Days of Poetry and Wine* (Medana, Slovenia) and *Feathers & Lime* (The Caseroom Press); in the periodicals *Far Off Places*, *Modern Poetry in Translation*, *New Books in German*, *PN Review* and *Shearsman*; and in the online journal *No Man's Land*. 'Search' was commended in the 2015 Stephen Spender Prize for poetry in translation, and published on *stephen-spender.org* and *theguardian.com*.

Our thanks go to the editors of all these publications.

Ken Cockburn is grateful for the award of a Creative Scotland Artist's Bursary, and for time spent as a Hawthornden Fellow, both of which enabled many of these translations to be made.